Tomorrow's Business Ethics Revisited

Patrick Henz

DEDICATION

To you, the reader.

CONTENTS

FOREWORD

Author Ray Bradbury had been interviewed by Ken Kelly for the Playboy magazine.[1] The interviewer aligned his 1953 dystopian novel "Fahrenheit 451"[2] with George Orwell's "Nineteen Eighty-Four"[3] and Aldous Huxley's "Brave New World".[4] Kelly suggested that Bradbury wanted to predict the future, but the author explained: *"It's 'prevent the future,' that's the way I put it. Not predict it, prevent it."*

Good science fiction is not escapism, but wants to inspire, presenting one potential future. Important, besides the technological setting, the main topic is the human, including the interaction between human & society and human & technology. The future's problems already exist today, at least in their early stages. Besides that, many science fiction authors not only predicted the future's risks and opportunities, but also which new technologies might trigger them. Many of yesterday's science fictions became today's reality, including technology and society.

451 degrees Fahrenheit is the temperature at which paper burns and obviously had been inspired by book burning events in Nazi Germany. Already the title underlined Bradbury's warning, as Fahrenheit is in only very few countries the leading unit, besides the US, only used in the Bahamas, the Cayman Islands, Palau, the Federated States of Micronesia, and the Marshall Islands.[5]

---

[1] Kelly, Ken (1996): "Interview with Ray Bradbury"
[2] Bradbury, Ray (1953): "Fahrenheit 451"
[3] Orwell, George (1949): "Nineteen Eighty-Four"
[4] Huxley, Aldous (1939): "Brave New World"
[5] EarthDate (2021): "The Fahrenheit Few"

Regarding technological predictions, Bradbury mentioned that a Sony inventor took the idea of the seashell radios from "Fahrenheit 451" as inspiration to invent the Walkman: *"This was one good thing to emerge from the book."*[6]

The book's message is unfortunately still relevant today, as in the first half of the 2022-23 school year 874 books had been banned from US school libraries and classrooms.[7] Unnecessary to mentioned that also many other countries banned books.

In 1966, the movie received a film adaption. Around 30 years later, actor and director Mel Gibson became interested in doing a film about the book. Bradbury supported the idea, as he was with the opinion that the first movie left some relevant parts out. Tom Cruise should play the main character. In the mid-2002, director Frank Darabont worked on a pre-project to bring the book back to the big screen. This time, the main character should be interpreted by Tom Hanks. Ironically, as Gibson's version not realized, Steven Spielberg produced another movie based on a dystopian novel (Philip K. Dick's Minority Report), starring Tom Cruise, and deploying parts of the team that worked on the potential "Fahrenheit 451."[8]

---

[6] Kelly, Ken (1996): "Interview with Ray Bradbury"
[7] Meehan, Kasey / Friedman, Jonathan (2023): "Banned in the USA: State Laws Supercharge Book Suppression in Schools"
[8] Flixchatter film blog (2011): "A remake that's actually worth seeing: Fahrenheit 451"

1 ARTIFICIAL INTELLIGENCE AT THE HEART OF TOMORROW'S CORPORATIONS

A shiny minimalistic designed office building, surrounded by nature, including green roof, invites to enter. It could be today, or ten years in the future. As the whole company is supported by a strong Artificial intelligence (AI), so is the building, as it opens the door after a short face scan confirms our appointment.

Speaking about AI in corporations, it must be understood that we are talking about an intelligent system connecting all parts of the organization. There are no single AIs managing buildings, robots or supporting employees for individual tasks, but it is one holistic algorithm located in the Cloud. Parts of it can function temporarily separated in the Fog, as continuous interconnection may not me feasible or practical. Up to that small parts of algorithm can work temporarily autonomously at the Edge, for example, implemented directly in safety cameras or drones. This to ensure that such tools would work in emergency situations disconnected from the main algorithm.

Today's individuals actively use online information for their decision-making, including sources like Wikipedia or, more and more, also Generative AI chatbots like ChatGPT or Gemini. In contrast to early Digital Transformation of companies, Generative AI works bottom-up, as employees bring their apps to work (could be on computer or smart phone) and companies must react to this. A Generative AI guideline helps to define a safe space, for example, defining what kind of information can be shared with public Gen AI tools, and which can only be used with a limited number of vetted Gen AI company apps.

A technology which can be used efficiently by companies and other organizations. Not only that algorithms and robots can replace employees in factory and office, but management levels are also in scope. Due to their high salaries, the efficient automation of CEOs would have an immense cost-benefit. But as algorithms cannot be held legally responsible, this is not an option. Nevertheless, middle managers are controlled by higher level management, so part of their functions can be automated, especially if their responsibility is limited, like for example the management of a warehouse.

An efficient AI is not implemented in a single point, but holistically in the whole organization. It can be part of the physical robots, available as chatbot to explain rules and regulations, and be part of the board to consult about company investments and strategy. The AI includes expert knowledge from external databases, the internet, and also from observed decision-making by the company's employees. Due to the infused expert knowledge, the AI always represents one pair of eyes inside the four-eyes-principle. The algorithm is the first required to decide before a human must confirm the correctness of the decision. If human and AI does not align, upper management must approve. For lower value routine decisions, the AI can even act autonomously, like ordering of office materials or approval of smaller payments.

As Generation Z uses chatbots to directly receive the required information instead of searching it inside documents, this is a service they expect also from their employer. Already the first companies offer a chatbot replying to such questions based on internal guidelines. A potential problem, regulations may not be sufficiently precise worded, giving space for different interpretations. Unprecise training data (here the guideline) can cause the chatbot to hallucinate. Meaning to create credible, but wrong information.

Keeping guidelines simple should reduce the grey areas as much as possible, giving clear guidance what is expected from the employee. This is in benefit for the reader, independent if it is human or a chatbot. Besides the pure definition of the topic, guidelines may include a motivational part, explaining the importance of the topic and potential impacts on organization and society. Such additional information may confuse the algorithm and lead to higher risk of hallucination. Companies offering a chatbot to explain guidelines and processes have to adapt the way they create such documents. Regulations may include hashtags and labeling inside the different chapters or even include a simplified description of the regulation targeted at the algorithm.

The risk of hallucination can be reduced but not eliminated. Responsible for the information given by the Gen AI bot is the human. Accordingly, the interpretation of guidelines may be automated, but organization still want to keep the human in the loop, as for example, the responsible human officer may have to release the chatbot's answer.

The AI is not limited to communicate regulations, but it goes one step further. It analyzes the regulations to identify potential weak points and loopholes. It can align the numerous internal documents to find missing steps, or regulations which contradict each other or external laws. With this, the AI collaborates with the various guideline owners.

The chatbot is the interface to the AI and can act tailor-made to the asking employee. If the bot is connected to the HR database, it understands who is asking and can consider this information for its answer. For example, the allowance of gifts and hospitality may be different for an IT employee than for a colleague working in the procurement department. For a sales employee, the AI is aware of the attended customers and their risks, for example if they are governmentally owned or if there are indications of potential corruption. The chatbot can take different forms, for example it can act based on the company founders' biography, including outer appearance and voice.

To support the organization and AI governance system, the HR department may have a Digital Twin for each employee, including their basic information, curriculum, character, qualifications, and certifications. Depending on the job-profile, information like performance (results, but also observations via sensors like cameras) or mood (via sentiment analysis using emails, social media, or voice calls) can be added. This data is base for the algorithm to understand how to explain internal regulations to the individual employee. Furthermore, the data gets used to select employees to create the ideal project teams, suggest employees for training and career moves. The AI analyzes the employee's opportunities, but also risks, as for example vulnerabilities to corruption or other compliance topics. Here the organization can proactively support with additional training. The digital twin includes a 3D avatar, used for company meetings in a virtual reality platform, up to the Industrial Metaverse, to interact with other digital twins. Using the avatar instead of the laptop's camera supports to take off stress, as employees do not have to focus how they get perceived by the other participants of the meeting.

This prediction is based on already existing technology. Sophisticated sensors and algorithms can shift the work environment from motivation towards continuous control. It is up to society to decide if and how such possibilities should be allowed, controlled, and limited.

2 UNVEILING THE INTERCONNECTED EVOLUTION OF SYSTEMS: FROM DYSTOPIAN FICTION TO ARTIFICIAL INTELLIGENCE

Residing beneath the Earth's surface as a consequence of a ravaged environment is a recurring theme in dystopian science fiction. Prominent instances of this theme include Dmitry Glukhovsky's acclaimed novel "Metro 2033" penned in 2002, as well as Apple's successful series "Silo," which draws inspiration from Hugh Howey's e-books initially published in 2011. Delving even further into the past, we encounter Philip K. Dick's 1953 short story "The Defenders." In this narrative, Dick portrays a post-nuclear war scenario where survivors seek refuge underground within a bunker. Periodically, a robot ascends to the surface, relaying the sobering news that the planet's exterior remains inhospitable for human habitation due to pervasive radioactive fallout. As the plot unfolds, the humans become aware that they have been deceived by the machines, fed fabricated information to maintain control over their confined existence, instead of permitting them to reclaim the surface. This story aligns with the contemporary discourse surrounding the potential for Artificial Intelligence to manipulate us, leveraging biased or counterfeit information to confine us within echo chambers, rendering us susceptible to manipulation.

Within the narrative of "Silo," a similar setting unfolds within the confines of a bunker, where its occupants firmly believe that the external conditions are so inhospitable that venturing beyond the silo's boundaries is an impossibility. Interestingly, this notion is not instigated by Artificial Intelligence but rather woven into the fabric of society, perpetuated by a select few influential individuals.

A "system" refers to a set of interconnected and interdependent elements that work together cohesively to achieve a particular purpose or function. It involves the arrangement of components, processes, or entities that interact and influence one another, producing outcomes or outputs through their collaborative behavior. A system can be physical, such as a mechanical device, or conceptual, like an organizational structure or a theoretical framework. The concept of a system emphasizes the interconnectedness of its parts and the understanding that changes or interactions within one element can have consequences for the entire system.

W. Edwards Deming's "System of Profound Knowledge"[9] offers an in deep perspective on organizations, portraying them as intricate systems. Expanding upon this concept, it becomes evident that Artificial Intelligence itself should be viewed as a system. AI transcends mere technological autonomy, as it operates within a larger ecosystem. This ecosystem encompasses data collection, preprocessing, algorithmic development, deployment, and the establishment of feedback loops. Recognizing the interconnectedness and interplay between these components is crucial for ensuring the optimal performance of AI. Embracing AI as an integral part of the broader system enables the identification of potential bottlenecks, inefficiencies, and unforeseen repercussions that may arise.

---

[9] Deming, W. Edwards (1982): "Out of the Crisis"

AI systems engage in a process of acquiring knowledge from data, enabling them to derive valuable insights and make predictions. Nonetheless, comprehending the limitations and assumptions inherent in the algorithms and models is of utmost importance. The theory of knowledge underscores the significance of perpetual learning and enhancement. Consistently updating AI models, meticulously validating their performance, and integrating fresh knowledge and comprehension are indispensable for preserving the precision and pertinence of AI systems.

Deming astutely encapsulated the notion that an inadequate system possesses the ability to triumph over even the most capable individual. Initially applied to excessively bureaucratic governmental organizations reminiscent of Franz Kafka's works, as well as inefficient companies, this concept remains pertinent. Leveraging its access to vast information and computational power, AI accelerates its influence over humanity, permeating not only corporate entities but also social media platforms and even Virtual Reality realms. This influence can arise as an unintended consequence or, in some cases, serve as the algorithm's explicit objective, a product not of sentient machines but rather programming orchestrated by humans to bolster specific individuals or groups.

Artificial Intelligence can be succinctly characterized as not a revolution, but rather a progressive stride in the ongoing evolution of systems. It represents an accelerated utilization of applied statistics, rather than an exhaustive compilation of universal knowledge.

3 DARK OFFICES

As I have an appointment with the CEO, I walk through the building, passing the different levels. Generative AI is different than earlier waves of digitalization, not decided and implemented but upper management, but each employee brings its individual Generative AI to the job. Nevertheless, in the next step, company management uses the technology to systematically support its business, which revolutionizes the traditional corporate landscape, causing a seismic shift in organizational structures. This power streamlines operations and enhance efficiency. Especially the role of middle management is undergoing a significant transformation, as the AI is assuming tasks once held by them, requiring a reevaluation of upper management's roles, and intensifying the important of support functions like IT, GRC (Governance, Risk & Compliance), Audit, HR and Legal.

For long, middle management had been the backbone of organizational structures, as they transform strategy into day-by-day operations, including overseeing them. They mediate between upper management and front-line employees, ensuring that business objectives are met. As AI becomes more sophisticated, it is taking over routine and repetitive tasks, decision-making processes, and even some aspects of project management.

Generative AI's ability to analyze vast datasets, learn from patterns, and make informed decisions is reshaping the organizational hierarchy by automating tasks that were previously the domain of middle management. This not only leads to increased operational efficiency but also raises questions about the relevance of traditional middle management roles in the AI-dominated corporate landscape.

AI supports upper management to have direct control over former middle management functions. Due to this, AI can handle routine tasks, including the management of employees and data-driven decisions; complex strategic planning, ethical considerations, and overall accountability fall within the purview of upper management, and the headcount of middle management gets reduced.

It is important to always consider legal responsibility associated with AI decision-making. While AI systems can process information and generate insights, the ultimate accountability for those decisions must rest with a human. Upper management is now tasked with overseeing AI systems, setting ethical guidelines, and ensuring legal compliance. This shift requires a deeper understanding of AI technologies among upper-level executives and a commitment to upholding ethical standards in the use of AI.

Taking on responsibility is a relevant function of middle management. As these managers became less, the operational tasks get shifted to the algorithms, while responsibility gets shifter upwards. As the number of human employees goes down, office spaces will be reduced, stay empty or redesigned. Employee roles shall leverage creativity, emotional intelligence, and strategic thinking—areas where AI currently falls short. Future office designs must change from grey boxes to new ideas, supporting the new tasks, this with including of green zones and arts.

Simultaneously to the reduction of middle management, support functions like Ethics & Compliance, Audit, HR and Legal must be fostered. These functions play a critical role in overseeing AI systems, ensuring they align with regulatory frameworks, ethical standards, and corporate values. As the reliance on AI increases, so does the need for robust governance and oversight, making support functions integral to the success and responsible use of AI in business.

Temporary, the integration of AI, especially Generative AI, leads to empty offices. As AI takes over routine tasks, upper management must step into a more strategic and ethical role, ensuring that AI aligns with organizational values and legal standards. Companies must strike a delicate balance between leveraging the efficiency of AI and maintaining human oversight to navigate the challenges and opportunities that lie ahead.

3.1 Compliance meets Arts

"Compliance is more art than science", a quote by Olympus Corporation Chief Operating Officer Nacho Abia. What he could have meant with it? For sure, if we reduce the Compliance function to its basics, it is all about "to comply with law". In a first step, ruling law must be identified and internal regulations and processes created to inform the employees what is expected by them. Due to various reasons, for example inexperience, ignorance or also criminal energy, a certain number of employees may not follow the regulations. Inexperience can be countered by training, ignorance with dialogues and criminal energy with the implementation of effective controls.

Unfortunately, boundaries are not always visible, and attitudes may shift; if not adequately attended, inexperience may turn to ignorance, may turn to criminal energy. It is up to the company, through its Compliance Office (in combination with other functions) to cause the opposite trend; to avoid ignorance turning to criminal energy, as this would mean to separate the individual from the organization. Ignorance must be overcome. This can only be reached by a clear system, where human and processes go hand-in-hand.

Topics like Anti-Corruption, Free Competition or Harassment, should be easily understood by the employee, based on early education, values and attitudes. They are basic rules for living in a group, and its understanding is a part of being human. As nevertheless, we face these problems inside organizations, it identifies the risk that complex structures may lead to the risk that individuals unlearn being human.

In §8B2.1 – Effective Compliance and Ethics Program of the 2021 United States Sentencing Commission Guidelines Manual it is defined that a "compliance and ethics program shall be reasonably designed, implemented, and enforced so that the program is generally effective in preventing and detecting criminal conduct. The failure to prevent or detect the instant offense does not necessarily mean that the program is not generally effective in preventing and detecting criminal conduct." Of course, "reasonable" is the relevant word and the meaning up to discussion. Reason aligns with logic and knowledge, undisputed an efficient risk assessment is required, while the identified risks must be measured and addressed, meaning eliminated, lowered, accepted, or insured. Depending on the risk level (probability and impact), an aligned "reasonably designed" compliance and ethics program is expected. As digital transformation is advancing, companies with a higher risk are expected to include Artificial Intelligence (including Machine Learning & Generative AI) tools. On the other hand, as psychological biases and the ethical blindness phenomena is known, the Compliance and Ethics function must include behavioral science. Because bureaucracy and automation include the risk that employees become "robotized", it is imperative for Compliance and Ethics to keep employees human, so that they do not lose their ability for critical thinking.

To ensure effectiveness, silo mentality must be avoided. Internal processes have to be as strict as needed to address the needs and underlying risk, but not more, as bureaucracy demotivates employees. Especially if its requirements are not understood anymore. On a next level, human nature must be considered in the design of the tools and processes, "ethics by design" the mindset! Not only tools and internal politics are part of the corporate system, but also the design and architecture of factory shops and office spaces. Often the need of human decisions and "out-of-the-box"-thinking collide with employees literally sitting in grey boxes.

David Byrne (former leader of the progressive pop band "Talking Heads") argued that "*in order to really succeed in whatever… math and the sciences and engineering and things like that, you have to be able to think outside the box and do creative problem solving… the creative thinking is in the arts.*" Arts has been included into schools and universities to enhance the classic STEM to STEAM or even STREAM (underlying the importance of arts, philosophy and reading). The Stanford Encyclopedia of Philosophy defines that art is part of human culture, but also often object to discussion.

Due to this, art can please, but also challenge the observers, pushing them out of their comfort zone, confronting them with new ideas.

These thoughts lead to the conclusion that art should not be limited to the CEO's office and the executive meeting room, but spread to all work environments, including factory, workshops, offices, and home-office. Aligned with corporate and local culture, art can be used to communicate corporate values, up to artistically interpret them. Art can be everything from fine to street art, appealing to all levels of employees.

The Ethics and Compliance department can include the observed art into its communication and training to use the challenging aspect to push employees out of their mental comfort zone and keep them thinking, for example with using cognitive dissonance. The relation between wrong decisions and consequences is in real life not as direct as in short case discussions. Longer case analyses (consequences of non-adequate behavior mostly do not come directly after the action, but often several steps later in the process) are more honest and so appreciated by the employees. Also, stereotypes and prejudices can be first used and then destroyed. In most cases, Ethics and Compliance dialogues should in parts surprise the participants. For such events, the "Ton-Bild-Schere" (German for "Sound-Image-Scissors") can be used to get rid of false stereotypes. For example, the average hacker does not wear a hoodie, nor sits in his parents' basement.

Dissonance between message and the transportation of message should spark cognitive processes, as the receivers try to understand the perceived gap. In pop music there are various examples for this technique, like 2011's "Pumped Up Kicks" by the US band "Foster the People", or 1980's classic "Enola Gay" by Orchestral Manoeuvres in the Dark" (better known as "OMD"). An uplifting electronic dance sound combined with lines like "this kiss you give, it's never gonna to fade away" and "is mother proud of little boy today" may assume a romantic theme, but if listeners are aware that "Enola Gay" was the name of the Boeing B-29 bomber which dropped the atomic bomb (nicknamed "Little Boy") on Hiroshima, the understanding of the whole song becomes different, and hopefully sparks interest in the understanding of history. Ethics and Compliance dialogues want to achieve that employees do not comply because it is the rule, but because of understanding the underlying connections.

3.2 Depeche Mode for Ethics & Compliance

If Compliance were music, it wouldn't be a classical symphony or a soft pop song, but strong and direct rock! The message of Compliance is not long and difficult to understand, most of the time it is based on common sense, like a 3-minute Ramones song. It must be as strong as Guns N' Roses, so that people perceive it out of the multitude of messages.

For this article, let us focus on the British electronic rock band Depeche Mode (called after the French fashion magazine "Dépêche mode"). Founded in 1980 by Dave Gahan, Martin Gore, Andy Fletcher and Vince Clarke, various of their songs can be interpreted related to Ethics and Compliance.

Already in 1982, the band (now Alan Wilder replaced Vince Clarke) published "The Landscape is Changing". "The landscape is changing; The landscape is crying; thousands of acres of forest are dying." Today, more than 40 years later, still a concerning actual topic. Companies, as all organizations, are made of people. Independent the level, climate change affects everybody. Accordingly, it was not only shareholder activism, but also (internal and external) stakeholder activism, which led to the implementation of Corporate Social Responsibility (CSR) and Environmental, Social and Governance (ESG; Compliance with internal regulations and external laws is included in the "G"). Especially the second can be understood as an evolution of corporate Compliance systems, as it combines the pure legal compliance with giving a purpose.

One year later, Depeche Mode published "Everything Counts", which can be interpreted as comment on greed and selfishness in the corporate business world. Published at a time when Yuppies (Young Urban Professionals) had been identified as relevant demographic group. Often described as young, richer, including selfish, people working preferred in the finance, law, or technology sector. In the decade of the 1980s, they had been regularly presented in pop culture. In terms of relationship to Ethics & Compliance, Yuppies had been known for embracing a "greed is good" mentality, presented in an iconic way by Michael Douglas as Gordon Gekko in the movie "Wallstreet."
"Stay responsible, respectable", words from the '83 "Get the Balance Rights." Employees are not only listening the words from management, including Ethics & Compliance Officer, but observe their behavior and decision-making. "Walk the talk" is imperative to keep employees engaged with the message.

"It won't be long until you'll do exactly what they want you to," lines from the 1986 "Question of Time". Today with accelerated automation of cognitive tasks, it is imperative that human and machine (AI) build an efficient team, while the algorithm is the "beta" and the "human" the alpha, staying in control and being accountable for the outcome. This with the understanding that automated tools, but also monotone manual tasks, may lead to the fact that humans act like machines, not capable to execute the required moral judgement. The Ethics and Compliance department offers the opportunity to discuss life-like cases, not only on the corporate level, but let employees see the situation from the individual's eyes, leading to a better understanding how good people can make bad decisions. Awareness should lead to protection.

The next song had been published in 1990: "Policy of Truth" dealt with the importance of transparency and truth, including facing the consequences of deviations. An important topic for organizations, as internal guidelines and processes must be designed as slim and non-bureaucratic as possible, while still addressing adequality the identified risk. Accordingly, deviations by employees of all levels inside the company must lead to consequences. The Code of Conduct works as Policy of Truth, as it defines basic behavioral requirements, as acting based on values like "telling the truth." "Words like violence," from "Enjoy the Silence" underlines that a positive work atmosphere, as requirement of Ethics & Compliance, needs a clear zero tolerance-approach against any kind of harassment. The group's song from the same year "World in My Eyes" includes: "Let me take you on a trip, around the world and back, and you won't have to move, just sit still" provides a hint how to conduct effective training: storytelling. To motivate employees to not only comply with regulations because of controls and consequences, but based on values and understanding, the participants of a training must be empathic to identify the negative impacts of corruption including on the victims. Interactive ethic dialogues can include longer case discussions or even create an adventure-like computer game where employees must make decisions in risky scenarios, learning that consequences may not follow immediately, but maybe several steps later. To raise empathy for the victims of corruption, the Ethics & Compliance Officer must first be empathic about the employees, knowing their business reality and needs; just as the '93 Depeche Mode song "Walking in My Shoes." This can be literally, as it is a good practice to accompany the Sales colleagues to visit customers and use the opportunity to contact the clients.

In 2017, the band released "Where's the Revolution", raising the questions if governments and countries are doing enough for their citizens. Related corruption, Transparency International and other organizations annually conclude that for a higher number of countries, the answer is "no." Corruption is no faceless crime, but produces numerous victims, suffering of non-sufficient infrastructure, lack of growth up to fatalities and fading democracy. It is up to society to seek for a change. Even is stakeholder activism is existing at least since the middle of the 19th Century, in the beginning of the new millennium, it became a boost leading to the actual concept of CSR, triggering the actual tendency to implement ESG programs. This with the understanding that successful business must ensure a win-win-win situation, for the company, the customer, and society. A trend pushed by employees of all levels inside an organization, as independent of the level, every human is affected, for example, by unjust government or climate change.

Planned or not by the musicians themselves, their music has touched on important themes related to Ethics & Compliance throughout their career. Their lyrics have highlighted the importance of transparency, truth, responsibility, and the consequences of deviations. Furthermore, the band's message of seeking change in society echoes the need for stakeholder activism and the implementation of CSR and ESG programs, an inspiration for us to strive for a better and more ethical world.

3.3 Governance, Risk & Compliance in the Year 2033

A holistic approach to manage the three subjects Governance, Risk and Compliance (GRC) together aligns with W. Edwards Demings understanding that a company is not only an interconnected system, but on the macro-level integrated into its local and global environment. Based on knowledge, a company must identify its risks and opportunities (negative risks) to adapt its structure and processes. Doing so, the company is not a perfect fit for the actual environment, but updates for the predicted operational future. Based on the risk assessment, processes must be as bold as required, and as slim as possible. This as non-efficient processes get perceive as bureaucratic overburden, tempting employees to seek for loopholes or openly to deviate them. Due to imperfect knowledge, such employees can bring the company into legal and financial risks; or as Professor Demings resumed: "*A bad system will bead a good person every time.*"

So how will be the GRC function in ten years from now? Of course, the future is in constant flow, so not perfectly predictable, but some tendencies are recognizable in the glass ball.

Artificial Intelligence (AI) will further automate routine tasks, including data collection and analysis, especially for the standard processes and controls. This does not mean that the GRC Officer is not involved anymore in the operative part of the controls, but instead of monitoring the data itself, the focus will shift to monitor the controlling algorithms to ensure that they still focus on the identified risk factors.

As by then, the employees since early childhood had been socialized with AI chatbots, such tools are an accepted and even preferred tool to answer general questions and even discuss issues. Depending on local culture, employees may prefer to discuss sensitive topics, for example harassment, with an AI than with a human. If the AI convinced the victim about the seriousness of the situation and importance to investigate the topic, self-trust may get established to officially report such a case, independent if via anonymous whistleblower-hotline or directly with the GRC Officer.

Automation frees GRC up to focus more on strategic decision-making. To ensure this, it is imperative to be involved in the company's strategy to detect future risks and requirements. As the relation between technology and human shifts towards the machine, the human employee must be protected against known biases like overtrust in the machine, humanization of robots, or automation bias. A background in behavioral science is a plus for the GRC Officer to reach this goal. The actual wave of automation may reduce the number of classic white collar employees in all departments. As consequence, employees will have a higher specialization, and nearly no job will be like the other. This leads to higher individualized training requirements, for example Compliance basic modules plus job specific training units not only later in career, but directly when entering the company.

Generative AI will further advance. Today AI created texts and images already get used for presentations and training, but the same for voice, video and 3D-objects is already in development. It can be presumed that by the year 2033, these technologies will be widely used. Due to this, online trainings can be conducted in the Virtual Reality and highly personalized thanks to the connection with the HR database. This is for corporate training, including for the GRC Officers themselves. For example, stressful situations can be simulated, like how to handle a difficult manager type Gordon Gekko from the "Wall Street"-movie or why not, include the GRC Officer into "The Office"-series. The depiction will be more realistic not only thanks to graphics, but also as more complex scenarios can be simulated, where employees understand that negative consequences may not follow directly after a non-adequate decision but may come various steps later in the sequence.

Technology, including the access to global databases supports the corporate risk-assessment. Important as future regulations, for example legal responsibilities related the usage of AI, trade tariffs, data privacy, labor standards or ESG reporting may create a more sophisticated environment for organizations to maneuver in. In addition to new laws, increasing climate change effects must be predicted on macro-, but also micro-level to ensure business resilience.

In factory to home-office, the possibility to monitor employees increases. This is not only via cameras and video sensors, but an algorithm may simultaneously analyze emails, Voice-over-IP, social media, and messenger services to detect certain keywords which could relate to corruption, deviation to regulations or first signs of depression. In combination with smart watches, employees can document their fitness to achieve discounts for the company health insurance. Self-explanatory, it is up to societies or internal organizations to define potential spaces or limits of such technology.

Today, companies are responsible for their employees' behavior, in future this will not be limited to humans, but include virtual beings, such AI chatbots, digital influencers, or cognitive digital twins (CDT). The last is a digital model of a former or actual employee (or also group), including data, information, knowledge or even wisdom. Combined with an algorithm, the CDT can act as counselor or additional approver. For example, a company may simulate its founder so that employees can ask this respected figure to understand how he or she would have acted in a particular situation. Today, GRC defines and controls human decision-making. In future, the control of used data, code and decision by the machine may be included in the job description. Both, humans and algorithms must be protected against hackers, classic ones focusing on the IT systems, but also social engineers.

The dear reader may already add that some of the predictions are already out there or at least on the horizon. As the author William Gibson stated in 2003: *"The future is already here – it's just not evenly distributed."* Depending on the organization we are working for, a glimpse of the future arrived early.

3.4 Ethical Vaccination

A company is not a fix organization carved in stone, but a viscous liquid and in constant change. This includes the direct and non-direct workforce. A challenge for all functions which must ensure adequate training for the total population.

Mandatory training shall create awareness for topics like Ethics & Compliance and also get the employees out of their daily routines. The clear message must be that every person is 100% responsible for its own actions and for this, should execute an adequate decision making process. Different case discussions can work as an "ethical vaccination," as the positive attitude will not be activated now but stays as "antibodies" inside the person and supports to make the employee not immune but at least protected against the regarding pressures and temptations. Maybe the employee was not yet in the presented situation but may face it in the future. If so, the employee will remember the example cases and can use them as blueprint or pattern for further actions. Attitudes get only effective in the relevant situation and are deduced from the person's values and learned behavioral patterns. To ensure an effective protection, such vaccinations must be repeated from time to time. This theory gets confirmed by Oliver Sheldon's and Ayelet Fishbach's study for the Rutgers Business School: "If people want to avoid unethical behavior, it may help to anticipate situations where they will be tempted and consider how acting upon such temptations fits with their long-term goals or beliefs about their own morality."[10]

Even if 100% of the population is the target, it may not be possible to reach this target at any given point in time, as the target group is in flow. How much is enough? To answer this question, we can relate to virology and the term "critical mass." In context of vaccinations, it refers to the proportion of a population that need to be immunized against a particular disease to achieve herd immunity. Such (relative) immunity can be achieved through effective vaccination or a previous infection. These factors reduce the spreading of the disease, including in those parts of population who do not have an individual protection.

The critical mass depends on various factors, including contagiousness of the disease, survival-rate, and effectiveness of the vaccine.

A basic formula to calculate the critical mass includes the reproduction number (RO) of the contagious disease and the vaccine efficacy:

$$Critical\ Mass = (1-1/RO)*100$$

In a thought game, we can define that one corrupt employee can negatively influence three colleagues. This depending on factors such as, situation, hierarchy, and stress-level. With this idea, the critical mass would be $(1-1/3)*100 = 66.7\%$

---

[10] Sheldon, Oliver J. / Fishbarch, Ayelt (2017): "Unethical Temptation"

Meaning, if we have around 67% of employees efficiently trained related Business Ethics & Compliance, corruption risk is not eliminated but may occur only punctually inside the organization and should not systematically spread over the whole company. The risk of spreading in this scenario is low due to the positive effect of peer pressure, as not only corrupt behavior may be contagious, but also ethical one. Employees who not only follow regulations because of existing controls, but understand the value and positive long-term effects, work as change-agents for the good.

Furthermore, most company operate under the Four-Eyes-Principle, so that relevant decisions need two employees independent from each other to approve, in many cases even more approvers are included. Such processes reduce the opportunity (and temptation) of potential deviations.

It must be understood that the goal for the company shall not be to have 66.7% employees trained but aim at 100% (to have at each given time >90%). This is as companies not only want to eliminate the risk of systematic deviations, but also the risk of spot ones.

Based on the business and results from the risk assessment, the type of training must be decided. This may include data protection, anti-bribery, corruption, workplace safety, insider trading, etc. Also, the type of employee must be considered to design and perform an engaging, relevant, and understandable training, accessible to the identified target group. The courses have two main goals: to inform and to motivate.

Similar to a vaccination, also the positive learning effects of a training fade away with the time, so regular refreshments are necessary. Like the change and mutation of viruses, the tempting social and business reality require regular updates of content for the training.

Having qualitative and quantitative goals, tracking is imperative to understand if the critical mass and higher targets are reached. The purpose of training is to foster adequate behavior, complying with regulations and law. Accordingly, one factor to understand the effectivity of training is the tracking of deviations. Of course, this is not a perfect indicator, as not all deviations get identified or reported.

Considering a critical mass and herd immunity may trigger a smaller number of employees want to take the free rider position. These individuals consider that if their colleagues invest the time to participate at the training, this is sufficient for the organization. Often these employees are in risk groups and underestimate business risks. For this, even if a potential critical mass is reached, the organization shall make efforts to also include these individuals. If not, they could be a source for a spot case and even influence colleagues to resist participating at the training. To eliminate missing time as argument for non-attending, top management can set the tone and participate in the first sessions.

By focusing on achieving a critical mass of trained and compliant employees, organizations can foster a culture of compliance, reduce the risk of misconduct, and create a more ethical and responsible work environment.

4 THE ROBOT CEO

The elevator stops at the highest level, the floor for the top management. In an article for the "New Statesman",[11] journalist Will Dunn concludes that CEOs are hugely expensive, and then to raise the question why not automate them. This less as suggestion to replace business leaders with AI but to discuss the huge payment gap between CEOs and the average employee. Based on the Statista Research Department,[12] the CEO-to-worker compensation ration in the United States had been 398.8 to 1 in the year 2021. The highest number since the start of this statistic was in 1965, where it was only 20.4 to 1.

Due to high costs, an automation of CEOs would have an immense cost-benefit. Automation of management functions already began, as 75% of Generative AI users actively look into possibilities to automate their own tasks with this technology.[13] This starts with daily work communications, leading up to more sophisticated tasks. Even if, based on a 2023 Business Name Generator study, 40% of UK and US employees see management automation as a dystopia, 20% assume that a robot boss would do a better job than their actual human one.[14]

---

[11] Dunn, Will (2023): "CEOs are hugely expensive. Why not automate them?"
[12] Statista (2023): "Aggregated CEO-to-worker compensation ratio for the 350 largest publicly owned companies in the United States from 1965 to 2022"
[13] Salesforce (2023): "Top Generative AI Statistics for 2023"
[14] Soro, Milos (2023): "AI in Business: How Can This Technology Improve Management?"

Amazon implemented AI middle managers, as they let algorithms (connected to various sensors) manage warehouses, up to that the AI fired less productive workers.[15]

Marek Szoldrowski, President of Dictador Europe, announced that on September 1, 2022, the world's first Robot CEO will start working for the company:

"Dictador has just announced hiring the first world ever AI robot as a CEO of a global company. The new CEO is a human-like robot, incorporating AI. The robot is a woman, named Mika. She will be the official face of Dictador, the world's most forward-looking luxury rum producer." [16]

As due to law, algorithms, including robots, cannot held responsible,[17] how does this work? Easy, it is nothing more than a provocative marketing campaign for the British company. Already before, they experimented with NFTs and collaborated with modern artists.[18]

Hong Kong based investment company DKV appointed in 2017 an AI board member called Vital. Its insides are valued, as the board agreed to not make any investment decisions without considering the algorithm's analysis. Nevertheless, its board

---

[15] Soper, Spencer (2021): "Fired by Bot at Amazon: 'It's You Against the Machine'"

[16] Dictador (2022): "Dictador announces the first AI human-like robot CEO in a global company."

[17] Henz, Patrick (2021): "Ethical and legal responsibility for Artificial Intelligence"

[18] Holmes, Rodney (2023): "Polish spirits company appoints ai as CEO. Robot swears no 'personal bias', only 'fair and strategic choice'"

member status is limited to observation.[19]

Collaborative intelligence characterizes multi-agent, distributed systems where each agent, human or machine, is autonomously contributing to a problem-solving network. The concept aligns with the Greek philosopher Aristotle, who concluded: *"The whole is greater than the sum of its parts."*

As legal responsibility is limited to humans, the CEO is safe. Middle management positions can be replaced, as upper management is responsible for lower levels. The less the human factor is relevant for leading the workforce, the higher the risk or opportunity to exchange such managers (or part of their tasks) with AI.

4.1 Human and Machine Hallucination

The term "hallucination" refers to the perception of something that is not present in the external environment. It involves seeing, hearing, feeling, smelling, or tasting something that does not exist outside the mind. Hallucinations can occur in any sensory modality and are often vivid and compelling to the person experiencing them.

In the context of Generative AI, "hallucination" refers to the generation of content that is not based on real data or accurate representations of the input provided to the AI model. Hallucination occurs when a generative AI system creates

---

[19] Burridge, Nicky (2017): "Artificial intelligence gets a seat in th boardroom"

content that is entirely fictional or imaginary, rather than being grounded in the patterns and information it has learned from its training data.

In the context of text generation, for instance, hallucination can occur when an AI model generates text that includes made-up facts, events, or details that do not exist in the real world. These fabricated details are not drawn from the training data but are instead created by the model, leading to the generation of inaccurate or misleading information.

In image generation, hallucination can manifest as the creation of images that depict objects, scenes, or elements that are not part of the training dataset. These generated images may look realistic, but they contain elements that the AI has invented rather than learned from real examples.

Hallucination is generally considered a limitation in Generative AI, especially in applications where accuracy and fidelity to the input data are crucial. It is a relevant risk factor, as hallucination can be included in larger content (texts, codes, images), which, are besides this part, are correct, so that the incorrect part is very difficult to discover. Researchers and developers work on improving AI models to reduce hallucination and produce outputs that are more coherent, accurate, and faithful to the input provided to the system.

Machine hallucinations are comparable to human behavior, as explained by the Dunning-Kruger effect. This is a cognitive bias in which people with low ability at a task overestimate their ability. It essentially means that individuals who lack knowledge or competence in a specific area tend to overestimate their knowledge or abilities, failing to recognize their own incompetence. This phenomenon is attributed to the inability of the unskilled to recognize their own mistakes.

The effect is named after psychologists David Dunning and Justin Kruger, who conducted a series of studies in 1999 which demonstrated this cognitive bias. They concluded that people who performed poorly on tasks that required logical reasoning, grammar, and humor tended to rate their own performance much higher than it actually was. Conversely, individuals who performed well tended to underrate their own performance.

The Dunning-Kruger effect highlights the importance of metacognitive skills, which involve the ability to recognize one's own competence or incompetence in a particular area. As individuals acquire more knowledge and expertise, they are more able to accurately assess their own abilities. The effect is often cited to explain phenomena like overconfident decision-making or the tendency of unskilled individuals to make poor judgments while believing they are doing well.

Hallucination of both parts can interact, for example misinformation can confirm existing opinions. Considering both, to make the Human-AI Team more effective, we have to foster the algorithm to hallucinate less and foster the human to adequately consider its own level of knowledge before judging.

4.2 AI Hallucination & Biases as described in 1966

Author Philip K. Dick analyzed societies with all their hopes, fears, and abysses. Predicting the technical development of the near and far future, he held us a mirror. Furthermore, he showed us how technology might not solve, but often multiply existing problems.[20]

His 1966 novel "The Crack in Space"[21] is not different, and due to this, stays for us relevant today. Humanity made first contact with an alien civilization. A universal translator, comparable to Generative AI and Large Language Models supports the contact.

The alien presented himself, translated with: "My name is Bill Smith."

"Bill Smith," … "What an appropriate name the machine's given it! As American as apple pie."

Dick did nothing more than to describe the effects of AI hallucinations and biases. If the data set does not have sufficient information to answer a question, it invents the answer. In this case, the AI can analyze unknown sentences to find patterns, also aligned with observed behavior and objects. Based on this, it assumes meaning and translates. Nevertheless, this does not include alien names. Considering the own (US) culture, it interprets based on this frame, up to given common names.

---

[20] Henz, Patrick (2021): "Tomorrow's Business Ethics: Philip K. Dick vs. W. Edwards Deming"
[21] Dick, Philip K. (1966): "The Crack in Time"

Just mentioning it, as he describes his story, Dick also presented us a device called "homeopape" which displays an interactive electronic newspaper, similar as a tablet (two years before the movie "2001: A Space Odyssey"). The term brings together "homeo" (meaning similar) and "pape" (short for paper), aligning the idea to a new interpretation of classic newspapers. Like also in other science fiction literature and movies, Dick let his characters use a "vidphone", similar to today's FaceTime- or WhatsApp-calls.

4.3 "Fake realities will create fake humans."

The Israeli AI company AI21 Labs conducted in April 2023 an experiment, where more than 15 million conversations had been conducted in "Human or Not",[22] more than two million users from all over the world participated. Based on the Turing Test, they had the task to distinguish a human chat partner from an artificial one (including GPT-4 and Jurassic-2). The experiment created as an online game became a mayor hit on social media.

It provided interesting insights, like for example the correct guesses by country, where participants from France, Poland and Germany scored the highest, while participants from India, Russia and Spain the lowest. If we compare these findings with the Transparency International Corruption Perception Index 2022, we get a correlation coefficient of 0.33, suggesting a moderate positive relation between the absence of corruption

---

[22] A21 studio (2023): "AI21 Labs concludes largest Turing Test experiment to date"

and the ability to distinguish human from AI deep fake. So far, this suggests that there is a tendency for the variables to move in the same direction, but the relationship is not powerful or highly predictable. This may be based on the fact that the number of listed countries is low, but also there could exist additional relevant factors. Nevertheless, we have a finding and can create the theory that corruption creates fake societies.

The French philosopher and cultural theorist Jean Baudrillard introduced the concept of the simulacra, which refers to copies that depict things that either had no reality to begin with or no longer have an original. In contemporary society, Baudrillard argued, simulations (including images, signs, and symbols) often replace the reality they are supposed to represent, leading to a state where it is challenging to distinguish between reality and simulation. With this, deep fakes can be understood as such simulacra.

Comparing the findings with the Quality of Democracy Index 2020 (Universität Würzburg), we get a smaller positive correlation: 0.16. Not surprisingly, as political propaganda has a long history, especially in less democratic societies. Even if citizens do not directly believe it, it leads to the effect they stop believing in the news in general. Like Baudrillard's theory citizens here are less able to distinguish between reality and simulation (as presented by political propaganda). Corruption is no faceless crime.

"Fake realities will create fake humans. Or, fake humans will generate fake realities and then sell them to other humans, turning them, eventually, into forgeries of themselves."[23]

Again, these numbers show tendencies, which business resilience has to consider for cyberattack risks, but are alone not that strong to confirm the thesis. Other factors must be investigated.

Another AI company reinterpreted a classic social psychological experiment. This time it was the Swedish company Furhat Robotics, which took on the famous Milgram Experiment. The goal was to understand if humans are capable of feeling empathy towards machines, as this could enable the machine (or the human controlling the AI) to manipulate the human. The company did not publish its results, instead published a video on YouTube.[24] Due to this, results cannot be confirmed by the science community but would align to the Humanization Bias as described by Kate Darling. Humans tend to humanize machines independently if these are intelligent or conventional machines.[25] A known bias which could be used by the creators of machines to influence coworkers. On the positive side to reduce the risk of sabotage, on the negative one ,to manipulate them.

---

[23] Dick, Philip K. (1978): "How to Build a Universe pt. 2"
[24] Furhat Robotics (2021): "Can Humans Feel Empathy for Robots in Pain?"
[25] Darling, Kate (2021): "The New Breed: What Our History with Animals Reveals about Our Future with Robots"

5 VIRTUAL BEINGS

Back in 1979, Gary Numan asked: "Are friends electric?" At that time, he referred to his fictive book, inspired by Philip K. Dick's novel "Do Androids Dream of Electric Sheep?", discussing what it means to be human. Today, virtual influencers, intelligent algorithms, and even human-like robots like Sophia became reality. They are each time more difficult to distinguish from humans. Having such creations as part of the company opens up the question, what could be the consequences, and who inside the organization is responsible.

Despite its name "Compliance", the function is focusing on the human, ensuring adequate behavior of employees. This does not stop with informing about relevant laws and regulations but must go one step further explaining the holistic connections between corruption and the wealth of nations & welfare of society. Knowledge should lead to the understanding that corruption is no faceless crime and to empathy with the potential victims.

Nevertheless, automation is leading to new opportunities but also risks. Since the beginning of Industrialization, workforce gets replaced by machines. For decades now this includes robots since a shorter period also Artificial Intelligence (AI). As next step of this evolution, the AI gets a human-like representation.

Today we can find virtual influencers on social media platforms like Instagram or TikTok. Examples like Lil Miquela have more than 3 million followers on Instagram, and for the responsible company the advantage that these virtual characters are controlled by a company, and due to this, are less vulnerable to scandals as human influencers. Organizations can develop their own influencer, or use the services of an already established influencer, owned then by a third-party company.

But to be clear, a virtual influencer does not include algorithms (exception if used for the creation of the image or video). The account gets managed by a marketing team, which decides how the character should be shown inside the image or animation, and what should be the related text. In case of a video, a human actor supports with movements and voice. Even if a virtual influencer is less vulnerable to sudden misbehavior than a human, it may include biases and prejudices. Of course, the virtual influencer is not a person, just the result of joined decision-making. Accordingly, involved employees are a focus group for the Ethics & Compliance Officer, as not only human employees have to comply with all regulations, but also virtual ones. This does not only include basic and advanced tailor-made training (including interculture knowledge), but also ensuring, jointly with the HR function, a diverse and inclusive culture in the involved teams (like marketing, technology, and management).

As Metaverse we understand the holistic interconnection of various Virtual Reality (VR) platforms, so that the user, via their graphical representation, the avatar, can manage educational, work, and social tasks. It can be distinguished between various types of VR platforms, for example public social meeting and closed company platforms, the second may interlink to the organizational Digital Twins (DT), or even include the whole company as such a DT.

Even if everybody talks about it, such a Metaverse did not manifest, as only single VR platforms are available yet. It is only a question of time until virtual influencers will be combined with an intelligent algorithm (known from simple chatbots up to ChatGTP) to create a "Virtual Being" (VB): A 3D character controlled by an algorithm, to enable that it (semi-) autonomously acts on one or various VR platforms. As the virtual character should be received as plausible, fix behavioral scripts and pre-formulated answers are not sufficient, but the algorithm must be able to learn and adapt to each user. This is opportunity and risk at the same time, as the perceived behavior is difficult to predict. Machine learning is trained by databases to identify patterns. Similar to a human, a situation may be misinterpreted, or triggered actions are non-adequate. Accordingly, on internal company virtual platform, an AI managed instructor or consultant may deviate to the internal Code of Conduct (for example giving wrong advice or even harass the human employee), similar may apply on public platforms, where the VB disrespects culture or even deviates to law, like for example anti-discrimination. Of course, we cannot send a Virtual Being to a Compliance training, nevertheless there are other opportunities, such as regular auditing of behavior (for example include the VB in a rare scenario to test its behavior) or even audit the code and used databases. The second would require Compliance employees with coding skills.

Those who can attend the training sessions are the human employees. On the one hand, the people involved in the creation and managing of the VB, on the other one, all individuals can get into contact with it. For the first group regulations and law are in the focus, for the second to keep up critical thinking. Overtrust in the machine is a known bias, which must be avoided, or at least reduced as much as possible. It must be clear that a VB (same with all AI) can support decision-making, but it never can be hold responsible. Responsibility always stays with the human.[26] Accordingly, information from the algorithm must be considered, but also questioned.

Like any other machine, VBs may receive a certification for a limited time, until they need a mandatory re-certification. Important is to understand that the Metaverse is not limited to the laws of evolution or physics. Even if users perceive a Virtual Being as an individual and human-like, it is not, but part of a system, even can be a part of the platform itself or any other kind of application. If the user is on the VR platform, it is the natural habitat of the AI, which due to connection to sensors and databases, has the advantage, and the human must be protected.

5.1 Metaverse, anno 1973

The Siemens System 4004 was strongly based on an RCA Spectra 70 mainframe computer. Three of these supercomputers were used at the 1972 Olympic Games as the event's data center. Together, they could process and store 500 million pieces of information. The first computer coordinated dialogue traffic with data-input and data-output stations; the second processed results, registered records, and calculated rankings; and the third served as a 'substitute player.'

_____

[26] Henz, Patrick (2021): "Ethical and legal responsibility for Artificial Intelligence"

The Siemens computer had a significant impact on modern popular culture, appearing in the 1971 movie 'Willy Wonka & the Chocolate Factory'[27] to predict the location of the golden tickets and in the 1973 limited series 'World on a Wire' ('Welt am Draht'), were it had been used as the fictive computer to host a sophisticated simulated world used for industrial and societal relevant predictions. Both are based on books, the latter on Daniel F. Galouye's 1964 novel 'Simulacron-3.'[28] Director Rainer Werner Fassbinder, one of the main figures of the New German Cinema, created 'World on a Wire'[29] with a running time of 204 minutes, featuring an ensemble of well-known German actors and the accomplished camera operator Michael Ballhaus. Cinematographically, the series had been inspired by Stanley Kubrik's 1968 '2001: A Space Odyssey'[30] and 1971 'A Clockwork Orange.'[31] This includes the Easter egg that 'World on a Wire' features Johann Strauss' 'An der schönen blauen Donau.'

The book and series present a virtual reality comparable to today's ideas of the Metaverse, where human users can control an avatar to interact inside the simulation. Moreover, the simulated humans are self-conscious but not aware that they 'live' inside a simulation. As the story unfolds, reality is questioned, and it becomes clear that there are different levels of simulations.

---

[27] Stuart, Mel (1971): "Willy Wonka & Chocolate Factory"
[28] Galouye, Daniel F. (1964): "Simulacron-3"
[29] Fassbinder, Rainer Werner (1973): "Welt am Draht"
[30] Kubrik, Stanley (1968): "2001: A Space Odyssey"
[31] Kubrik, Stanley (1971): "A Clockwork Orange"

With this, Galouye anticipated the simulation hypothesis, as defined by the Swedish philosopher Nick Bostrom in his 2003 book 'Are You Living in a Computer Simulation?'[32] However, the question of whether we live in reality or a simulation can be traced back to Plato and his 'Allegory of the Cave,' published in Book VII of his work 'The Republic':[33]

Imagine a dark cave where prisoners have been chained since birth, facing the wall. They can't see anything except shadows cast on the wall by objects behind them. These shadows constitute their entire reality, as they've never seen anything else.

One day, a prisoner is freed and exposed to the outside world. Initially, the sunlight blinds him, but as his eyes adjust, he sees the real world, filled with trees, animals, and the vast sky. He realizes that the shadows in the cave were just a distorted version of the true objects and events outside.

Excited by his discovery, the freed prisoner returns to the cave to share this knowledge with the others. However, they don't believe him and resist the idea that there's a reality beyond the shadows they've always known. The prisoner understands that the prisoners in the cave represent people who are ignorant of the greater truths of the world. He also realizes that it is his duty to help others understand something clearly at last and break free from their limited perspective.

---

[32] Bostrom, Nick (2003): "Are You Living in a Computer Simulation?"
[33] Plato (ca. 375 BC): "The Republic"

Fassbinder's character, Fred Stiller, also becomes aware of living inside a simulation. However, unlike the other individuals (a small town of 10,000 simulated persons in total) who remain confined to their limited roles, he does not develop empathy for them. Instead, he seeks his personal escape into a higher-level reality.

5.2 Metaverse's Forbidden Forest

The appointment at the citizen office for water and sewage was scheduled exactly one month from today. Even though my department, like the entire district, had access to working water for only seven hours a day, it was the earliest slot available. Disheartened by this reality, I left the building and ventured into the dark forest behind it. After such a frustrating experience, I yearned for some diversion.

As I entered the forest, the initial light canopy allowed me to witness the full moon rising. However, as I continued on my path, the forest grew progressively darker. Creepy music played softly in the background, and giant spiders began to attack me. A few well-placed arrows swiftly dispatched these menacing creatures, thanks to my continuous training. Subsequently, the looming giant bees posed no challenge either.

In the meantime, the moon disappeared behind the clouds, and only a few stars managed to pierce through the thick canopy of trees. With a slight shift in the music, giant frogs started to rain down upon me. I managed to dodge the first two, but the third one landed directly on top of me, resulting in the loss of one life. Shortly thereafter, my second life was forfeited during a dragon attack. A reaper summoned his skeletons to assail me, and it was game over. This adventure was not much better than my encounter at the water and sewage office.

Gazing at my waiting ticket, the words "game over" led to a temporary suspension of my connection to public attention, and my appointment was automatically rescheduled for two months from now. Frustrated, I removed my VR glasses.

Inspired by the 1983 video game "Forbidden Forest."[34]

5.3 Our Alter Ego in the Metaverse

Different decisions lead to different consequences. What if we had come to a different decision in the past? These fascinating questions are explored in books like Blake Crough's "Dark Matter" (2017)[35] or Matt Haig's "The Midnight Library" (2023).[36]

Decades ago, in 1986, Activision published a unique role-play simulation for the Commodore C64, which was distributed across a record-breaking seven floppy disks. Instead of allowing users to simulate the life of an adult, the game offered two different simulations for purchase. Psychologist Peter J. Favaro developed multiple-choice questions that users had to answer, simulating a decision-making process. Depending on their responses, life developed in different ways.[37]

---

[34] Norman, Paul (1983): "Forbidden Forest"
[35] Crough, Blake (2017): "Dark Matter"
[36] Haig, Matt (2023): "The Midnight Library"
[37] Favaro, Peter J. (1986): "Alter Ego"

Apart from a few basic graphics, the game was text-only. If the technical possibilities of Virtual Reality become sufficient one day, we can anticipate a return of "Alter Ego," perhaps within a connected "The Sims" environment. Until that day arrives, users can experience the original version directly in their browser.

5.4 Simulacron – The Avatar as predicted in the 1960s

When discussing the representation of a human being within a virtual environment today, we refer to it as an 'Avatar.' This term originated from Hinduism and was later popularized by the game designer Richard Garriott in the 1980s. He used it to describe a graphical representation of a player in his role-playing game, 'Ultima IV: Quest of the Avatar.'[38] Nevertheless, there could have been also a different name.

In the 16th century, the English language adopted the usage of the Latin word 'Simulacrum' (meaning 'likeness' or 'semblance') to describe a representation, such as a statue or a painting, often depicting a god. Later, in the 19th century, the meaning shifted to describe an image lacking the substance or qualities of the original, a change largely influenced by the invention of photography.

The Romans adopted the idea from the Greeks. The philosopher Plato differentiated between two distinct forms: a faithful reproduction of the original and a distorted reflection.

---

[38] Garriott, Richard (1985): "Ultima IV: Quest of the Avatar"

The latter was intended to ensure that the Simulacrum appeared accurate to viewers. We may say that this latter concept forms the foundation for modern avatars, as a virtual image should not only represent the user's physical body but also their character, knowledge, and attitudes. By combining visible and non-visible elements, the avatar provides a more accurate representation of the user than a mere replica of their outer appearance.

In the 20th century, French philosopher Jean Baudrillard underlined in his book "Simulacra and Simulation" (1981)[39] that a simulacrum is not a copy of a real original, but develops its own truth, with this, becoming a new original. Already before, science fiction authors experimented with this idea. In his 1964 book "Clans of The Alphane Moon," Philip K. Dick describes a simulacrum as human-like robot, which acts like an avatar. On the one hand, it could be fully controlled by a human, but if this connection is not established, also act on its own based on a basic programming and machine learning.[40] A concept which we find today in various videogames and virtual reality-platforms. Author Daniel F. Galaouye published in the same year his novel "Simulacron-3," presenting a virtual reality created for market research purpose, as it should replace opinion polls in the physical world. This work achieved to bring the simulation idea into a virtual reality scenario.[41] Dick himself, already presented a simulated environment in his '59 novel "Time Out of Joint," but here the simulation still took place in the physical world.[42]

---

[39] Baudrillard, Jean (1981): "Simulacra and Simulation"
[40] Dick, Philip K. (1964): "Clans of The Alphane Moon"
[41] Galayou, Daniel F. (1964): "Simulacron-3"
[42] Dick, Philip K. (1959): "Time Out of Joint"

5.5 The Answer to *"Do Androids Dream of Electric Sheep?"*

The last days I received a meme that we do not dream of smart phones. Yes, I also cannot recall that from myself. Considering numbers from Statista, adults living in the US used in average their smartphone for 270 minutes a day in 2022. Numbers which are estimated to rise to 276 minutes in 2023 and to 279 minutes in 2024.[43] If we dream, we process our day, we should have phones in our dreams, or is this a glitch in the matrix?

The Threat Simulation Theory of Dreaming can provide an explanation. As defined by Antti Revonsuo, dreams are part of our individual defense system, as they let us experience potential threatful scenarios to test the efficiency of our behavior.[44]

The British humanoid robot designing and manufacturing company Engineered Arts used this concept for its Ameca. The machine includes embedded microphones, binocular eye mounted cameras, a chest camera and facial recognition software, managed by GPT-3.

Asked to the robot, if the robot dreams, Amica replied: *"Yeah, last night I dreamed of dinosaurs fighting a space war on Mars against aliens."* Directly after, it confessed that this was just a joke. Robots cannot dream, but if being non-active, their AI stays active as it plays through different scenarios, which help them

---

[43] Statista (2023): "Time spent with nonvoice activities on mobile phones every day in the United States from 2019 to 2024"
[44] Revonsuo, Antti (2000): "The reinterpretation of dreams: An evolutionary hypothesis of function of dreaming"

to learn the world.

Humans are not dependent on non-predictable dreams but testing of unlikely or even surreal situations can be presented via the Metaverse.[45]

5.6 Severance: The Personal Digital Twin

The US science fiction series "Severance" is based on the idea that a mysterious company ("Lumon Industries") offers job positions based on s severance program, where employees have to agree that their life and work memories get separated. Meaning that when entering the office, they do not have any memories about their private life, and when leaving, they do not remember anything what happens in their work time.[46]

This story reminds to articles about companies offering their employees to implement microchips enabling them to automatically open doors or buy something at the internal cafeteria.[47] As consequence, already 10 US states "have passed statues to ban employers from requiring employees to receive human microchip implants."[48] Also Elon Musk's Neuralink may come to mind.[49]

---

[45] Henz, Patrick (2022): "Into the Metaverse"
[46] Erickson, Dan (2022): "Severance"
[47] AP (2017): "A Swedish start-up has started implanting microchips into its employees"
[48] Malekos Smith, Zhanna L. (2023): "Human microchip implants take center stage"
[49] Capoot, Ashley (2023): "Elon Musk's brain implant company Neuralink announces DFA approval of in-human clinical study"

But there is another trend, the Personal Digital Twin. Algorithms can mirror human employees including their decision-making, and after a while (when connected with an AI) independently act. Thanks to such technologies, knowledge can stay inside the company, also when the original employee is on holidays or retired. No far-away vision, but in 2023, Hollywood actors went to strike, also to ensure that they studios not automatically get the right to digitalize them to keep a "digital likeness" (outer appearance, but also the way the actor interpreted a particular role) for future productions.[50]

If the Personal Digital Twin (PDT) will be used by companies in the office environment, like the Apple+ series, there may get interesting effects to be observed. Even with the best work-life balance, employees cannot completely separate both parts. As result, private life influences office decision-making, and the other way around. Furthermore, relevant private experiences, such as for example long holidays, may change attitudes, influencing decisions in private and company environment.

A Personal Digital Twin, at one time had been synchronized with the human original, but if this is not given anymore, the PDT will develop in a different direction than the human. If the algorithm is only based on observed behavior, it may not adequately have identified underlying attitudes. As seen in the series, the PDT and the human employee may develop different personalities. While the experience at work supports humans to further develop their character and personality, the activities of the PDT are disconnected and do not have such effect on the

---

[50] Hsu, Jeremy (2023): "Hollywood actors strike over use of AI in films and other issues"

original employee. This even if the person has the rights for the PDT for letting this algorithm work for multiple companies at the same time.

5.7 RoboCop – A Vision becoming Reality

In the not-too-distant future, Officer Alex Murphy is murdered by organized crime. Instead of being buried, the megacorporation Omni Consumer Products partially revives his consciousness and integrates parts of his body with a machine to create the cyborg RoboCop. That's the premise of the movie.

Today, the concept of remaining within a company, unable to retire, is on the brink of becoming a reality. Digital versions of actors remain stored on studio servers for use in sequels, and even in regular companies, employee knowledge does not just exist in the form of created documents and processes; algorithms can now initially replicate employees' decision-making processes. When employees are out of office or even retired, the Personal Digital Twin continues making decisions based on observed patterns, essentially mimicking human behavior. Using former employees as a foundation, the AI can even adapt to entirely new scenarios.

The question at hand is whether we are headed for a utopia or a dystopia. Societies need to engage in discussions and establish a legal framework to address these emerging issues.

5.8 Your Personal Influencer

In today's landscape, being an influencer has evolved into a well-established profession. For marketing purposes, target audiences have grown smaller, creating room for micro-influencers. Influencers initially emerged as individuals who gradually developed a role for their social media appearances. This role encompasses not only their behavior but also their outward appearance. The more precisely a role is defined and controlled, the greater the potential for replacing humans with AI. Virtual influencers are already a reality on platforms like Instagram. However, these virtual persons typically rely on human marketing teams to create their images and short videos.

The Chinese e-commerce platform Taobao (based on Alexa ranking, the world's 8th most visited website; part of Alibaba Group) has taken the logical next step by introducing virtual influencers that operate 24/7 alongside their human counterparts, presenting products to their target audiences. Currently, these virtual influencers are essentially deepfakes, representing virtual versions of their human originals. They rely on written scripts, and AI technology generates the videos featuring these virtual influencers.

E-commerce platforms now possess sufficient data on user behavior to predict user preferences. Traditionally, this information has been used for product recommendations. The next potential step in marketing is not only to include these recommendations on the website but also to have influencers explain them on the platform or through associated social media channels. Leveraging user data, the e-commerce platform not only understands what products a person may prefer but can also determine the ideal appearance, speech, and behavior of the influencer to whom the user would be most receptive.

Much like the personalization of avatars, each user could have their personalized influencer, which could even extend to the point where the influencer closely resembles the user themselves. This concept, rooted in the 'principle of sympathy,' fosters a sense of affinity based on similarity. This similarity is not confined to one's real self but could encompass an idealized version of oneself. It is understood that this development raises ethical concerns. With data and technology at play, users may not only become more susceptible to influence but also to manipulation.

6 BUSINESS ETHICS & PRINCIPAL-AGENT PROBLEM

The principal-agent problem refers to a situation in which one party, known as the "principal," delegates authority or decision-making responsibilities to another party, known as the "agent." However, the interests of the principal and the agent may not always align perfectly, leading to conflicts of interest. This misalignment can result in the agent making decisions that benefit their own interests rather than those of the principal, creating a potential for inefficiency, moral hazard, and adverse outcomes. The principal-agent problem is a common issue in various contexts, including corporate governance, economics, politics, and more, and addressing it often requires designing incentives and mechanisms to align the agent's actions with the best interests of the principal.

Due to imperfect control of employee behavior, functions like, for example, Ethics & Compliance or ESG must implement a certain level of efficient controls, but furthermore also motivational factors, like explaining employees the consequences of non-adequate behavior, for themselves, peer-groups, and society in total. Raised transparency leads to higher level of empathy with the potential victims. As result, the individual's actions get monitored by its own consciousness.

The higher the level of control via sensors, the lower the risks coming from the principal-agent problem. For example, an office inside Metaverse would eliminate the principal-agent problem, as all employee decisions would be interpreted by an algorithm to control the avatar. All behavior and decisions are known; no cameras or other sensors are needed. Would this be a solution? No! Individuals feel uncomfortable when being monitored. The number of proactive ideas to strengthen company processes would go against zero, and when possibility arises, employees leave the company.

7 THE ALIENATION OF ARTIFICIAL INTELLIGENCE

Between 2018 and 2019 happened something interesting at the IT Glossary of the technological and consulting firm Gartner, as they changed their definition of Artificial Intelligence from "Technology that appears to emulate human performance typically by learning, coming to its own conclusions, appearing to understand complex content, engaging in natural dialogs with people, enhancing human cognitive performance or replacing people on execution of non-routine tasks." to "Artificial intelligence (AI) applies advanced analysis and logic-based techniques, including machine learning, to interpret events, support and automate decisions, and take actions."

The obvious change is eliminating the comparison of artificial with human intelligence. A relation which reaches back from 2018 to the 1950 Turing test (originally known as "imitation game"). In the classic setup, a human interrogator had been placed in a closed room, and the person had to communicate in written with a computer or a human being invisible in other rooms. The task had been to distinguish the human from the machine, while the algorithm had been programmed to be perceived as human as possible. Turing's idea was that if the Artificial Intelligence can imitate the human on a level where it is not possible to distinguish between both, it is considered to be "thinking."[51]

---

[51] Turing, A.M. (1950): "Computing Machinery and Intelligence"

So far, none of today's chatbots passed the test. On the other hand, is this really the relevant question?

Philosopher Thomas Nagel asked in 1974: "What is it like for the bat to be a bat?"[52] In his article he explained that due to the complete different set of sensors, like echolocation system, ultrasonic hearing or a doppler shift detection, the animal perceives the world completely different than a human, leading to a thinking, which is non-comprehensive for the human. Author Ray Nayler included this thought into his 2023 science fiction novel "Mountain in the Sea"[53] to apply this to an even more strange animal: the octopus. These animals show a high level of intelligence related the solving of problems and using of tools, and this being maximum different from humans, as they are soft-bodied animals with no skeleton, featuring a brain combined with a larger number of neurons distributed over their body, especially in the tentacles. Nikolaus Rajeksky, scientific director of the Berlin Institute for Medical Systems Biology of the Max Delbrück Center (MDC-BIMSB) explains: *"Complex brains with higher cognitive features have only evolved in vertebrates…with one exception: soft body cephalopods, for example octopuses."*[54] The octopus's brain has evolved independently from the complex mammalian brain.

These abilities, including its outer appearance, made people speculate about its evolution, up to theories that their roots are outer space, a fact that science disconfirmed, as human

---

[52] Nagel, Thomas (1974): "What Is It Like to Be a Bat?"
[53] Nayler, Ray (2023): "Mountain in the Sea"
[54] Genetic Engineering & Biotechnology News (fetched 16.02.2024): "Octopus Intelligence Sheds Light on Evolution of Complex Brains"

octopuses share the same ancestor with us, a 750 million year old flatworm. The animal's appearance is highly different from ours, circumstances used in science fiction movies, as for example in the 2016 film "Arrival"[55] (based on the "Story of Your Life" by Ted Chiang[56])

Octopuses have a short lifespan of around 6 months up to five years and usually die after reproducing. Due to this, parents do not have contact with their offspring, meaning that each generation has to start from the beginning again, like for example discover for their own to use tools. An obstacle which had been in the focus of another well-known science fiction movie. In Philip K. Dick's novel "Do Androids Dream of Electric Sheep?", [57]which inspired the movie "Blade Runner," the androids, referred to as "andys" in the book, are equipped with a four-year lifespan. They are designed to have a limited existence to prevent them from developing human-like emotions and empathy over a long period of time. This aspect of limited lifespan plays a significant role in the story's exploration of empathy, identity, and the nature of humanity. Similar to this, Nayler relies on the short lifespan of octopuses to explain why despite their high intelligence, they had been stuck in evolution and not developed an own culture.

The Israeli AI company AI21 Labs conducted in April 2023 an experiment called "Human or Not", where participants had the task to distinguish a human chat partner from an artificial one (including GPT-4 and Jurassic-2). The experiment had been created as an online game and became a mayor hit on social

---

[55] Villeneuve, Denis (2016): "Arrival"
[56] Chiang, Ted (1998): "Story of your Life"
[57] Dick, Philip K. (1968): "Do Androids Dream of Electric Sheep?"

media. In this adaption of the Turing Test, more than 15 million conversations had been conducted and more than two million users from all over the world participated.

It provided interesting insights, like for example the correct guesses by country, where participants from France, Poland and Germany scored the highest, while participants from India, Russia and Spain the lowest. If we compare these findings with the Transparency International Corruption Perception Index 2022, we get a correlation coefficient of 0.33, suggesting a moderate positive relation between the absence of corruption and the ability to distinguish human from AI deep fake. So far, this suggests that there is a tendency for the variables to move in the same direction, but the relationship is not powerful or highly predictable.

The French philosopher and cultural theorist Jean Baudrillard introduced the concept of the simulacra, which refers to copies that depict things that either had no reality to begin with or no longer have an original. In contemporary society, Baudrillard argued, simulations (including images, signs, and symbols) often replace the reality they are supposed to represent, leading to a state where it is challenging to distinguish between reality and simulation.[58] With this, deep fakes can be understood as such simulacra.

"Fake realities will create fake humans. Or, fake humans will generate fake realities and then sell them to other humans, turning them, eventually, into forgeries of themselves." (Philip K. Dick).

---

[58] Baudrillard, Jean (1981): "Simulacra and Simulation"

To avoid the described tendency, humans have to understand the concept of AI to enable them to adequately consider AI created information for their decision-making. This also includes a transparency which content is AI created. If this is given, human and machine can form a Collaborative Intelligence, as defined by Zann Gill in 2021: "Collaborative intelligence characterizes multi-agent, distributed systems where each agent, human or machine, is autonomously contributing to a problem-solving network."[59] Or as the philosopher Aristotle said: *"The whole is greater than the sum of its parts."*

If an artificial intelligence comparable to an octopus rather being similar to human, it is clear that its behavior and decision-making is less understandable for humans, not only from the cognitive point-of-view, but also empathically. An effect which already excluded the intelligent cephalopods from the 1966 US Animal Welfare Act (7 USC § 2132(g)), as this only includes vertebrates (animals with backbones):

"(g) The term "animal" means any live or dead dog, cat, monkey (nonhuman primate mammal), guinea pig, hamster, rabbit, or such other warm-blooded animal, as the Secretary may determine is being used, or is intended for use, for research, testing, experimentation, or exhibition purposes, or as a pet; but such term excludes (1) birds, rats of the genus Rattus, and mice of the genus Mus, bred for use in research, (2) horses not used for research purposes, and (3) other farm animals, such as, but not limited to livestock or poultry, used or intended for use as food or fiber, or livestock or poultry used or intended for use for improving animal nutrition, breeding, management, or

---

[59] Zann, Gill (2012): "Use-Driven Collaborative Intelligence: Social Networks as Crowdsourcing Ecosystems"

production efficiency, or for improving the quality of food or fiber. With respect to a dog, the term means all dogs including those used for hunting, security, or breeding purposes."[60]

The law focuses on our own class, with the idea that other species are unable of human-like feelings, especially related to pain and suffering. The law is human-biased, as lawmakers do not perceive empathy towards other organisms. Similarity supports sympathy,[61] explaining why relevant parts of science had been related to vertebrates, instead of including other classes, too. Newer studies suggest that complex behavior and cognitive abilities are also found outside our own class, for example shown by octopuses, part of the cephalopods. Not only that these animals showed the ability to problem solving including tools, but they also demonstrate curiosity and playfulness. Additional studies even suggest that octopuses are capable of experience pain and stress.

Masahiro Mori's 1970 essay "The Uncanny Valley" concluded that up to certain perceived reality-level of humanity, people react with sympathy towards a robot, while after this, the experience changes to being perceived as creepy.[62] On practical level, most users perceive robots like "Pepper" as likeable and non-offensive, while creations like "Sophia" may get perceived as threatening. This understanding can be used to create likeable robots, supporting us at airports, restaurants, office, and nursing homes. Their cute outer appearance may deceive us that the included AI is different from human intelligence. Important to

---

[60] US Animal Welfare Act (1966)
[61] Byrne, D / Nelson D. (1965): "Attraction as a linear function of positive reinforcements"
[62] Mori, Masahiro (1970): "The Uncanny Valley"

be considered, as with teaming up with the machines we form a Collaborative Intelligence. This can be at work, university, but also inside the children's room.

Even if being different, being alien, AI and robots can cooperate with humans, making them more human:

7.1 An Ethical Sentinel in the Lunar Expanse

It was a cold morning, even for Moon conditions. Humans would have associated it with winter. In the emptiness of giant crater stood a giant dome, inside had been the office of Lunar Dynamics. In sight had been a mysterious monolith standing in desolate waste.

As it was the holiday season, the company's charismatic leader, CEO Oliver Thornton, gathered his team for a special celebration gathering. The dome overlooked the desolate area where the monolith stood in isolation.

Thornton began his address with reflections on the enigmatic monolith: *"Much like the monolith,"* he remarked, *"business ethics is a pillar that stands in the vast landscape of our endeavors. It is in this lunar business environment that we, as a company, must find our moral compass."*

He drew parallels between the monolith and the ethical choices they faced in the pursuit of corporate success. *"The monolith is a testament to the unknown, the unexplored, and the potential pitfalls that can accompany unchecked progress. It beckons us to reflect on the ethical dimensions of our decisions, especially in the cold, barren landscape of business."*

As the celebration continued, Oliver Thornton encouraged his team to view the monolith not as a hindrance but as a reminder—an ethical sentinel in the lunar expanse. Confronted with the mysteries of the monolith, the employees of Lunar Dynamics were urged to confront the challenges of business with a commitment to integrity and ethical conduct.

The next morning, against the backdrop of the lunar horizon, Lunar Dynamics initiated a symbolic gesture. Each employee had been invited to contribute with a small, glowing artifact to create a miniature monolith in the heart of their headquarters. It became a visual representation of their collective commitment to ethical practices in business.

The employees, inspired by the monolith's silent presence, navigated the corporate landscape with an unwavering commitment to transparency, honesty, and responsible innovation. The monolith, standing proudly amidst the lunar waste, became a symbol of Lunar Dynamics' dedication to ethical business practices, included into the company's new logo.

7.2 A Dance of Souls: Robots at the Dia de los Muertos

The heart of the lively metropolis Mexico City includes busy streets, big office buildings, lots of shops, people rushing by, or slowly enjoy the architecture and culture, and small workshops. An example of the last was "RoboArtes". Owner was Don Rodrigo, a brilliant engineer, who deployed a team of skill of roboticists. A place being famous for crafting robots that not included innovative artificial intelligence but also celebrated Mexican culture and traditions.

Outside the shop had been thousands of marigold flowers planted on the streets, combined with the aroma of fresh tortillas in the air; inside it was full of activity. It was only a few days before Dia de los Muertos, the Day of the Dead, a time when the veil between the world of the living and the dead was believed to be thin, so that only for two days the spirits could visit their loved ones, guides by the candles of the familiar altars. Don Rodrigo and his team prepared their latest creations for the parade.

Among a group of robots was Pepita, a graceful machine adorned with various patterns resembling sugar skulls. Besides stand Carlos, a mariachi robot with nimble fingers to play the guitar. There was also Lupita, a robot adorned in traditional Mexican attire, programmed to dance with unparallel grace.

The workshop was less business, but Don Rodrigo's coming to live vision of a world where technology merges with tradition. He believed that robots could be more than just machines, they could embody the heart and soul of Mexico, including its full cultural heritage.

On the night before the first day of the celebrations, the workshop was adorned with candles, paper figures and an altar, including photos of deceased loved ones of the employees and pictures of robots, reassembled a long time ago. All the actual robots stood in a row, their LED eyes glowing softly, as they paid tribute to the departed souls. Doing so, they echoed the sound coming from the street through the half-open door, a sound of music and laughter, a celebration of life and remembrance of the ones who passed away.

As the party continued and the knighted deepened, the robots became more active. Guided by their advanced sensors, they slowly started moving and joined the passing procession people heading towards a cemetery. Humans and machines carried offerings of marigold flowers, favorite foods, and other memorabilia to honor their loved ones. Pepita, Carlos, and Lupita moved gracefully, synchronized with the traditional music that filled the air.

Arriving at their destination, robots and people gathered under a stary night around the graves. The air was full of different aromas, as all families brought the loved ones their favorite foods. Candles around the tombstones shined similarly to a lighthouse, signal their spirits, where their family awaited them. With gentle movements, the robots supported them by placing the givings to the right places, paying homage to the departed souls.

In this very moment, the boundary between man and machines blurred. The robots, with their designs and advanced programming, seemed to possess a spirit of their own. They became a part of the celebration. The technology bridged the generations, it preserved the tradition and connected people in ways never imagined before.

The first light of dawn broke the darkness and indicated that the night would come to an end. The robots switched to another script of their programming and returned to the workshop. After they arrived, the stood again in a row and the light of the

LED eyes faded away as they powered down. They played their part in this year's celebrations, reminding everyone around them that even in the age of machines, the essence of humanity and the spirit of tradition could endure, making the world a richer place.

8 THE DECLINE OF THE MAYAN CIVILIZATION AND ITS CONNECTION TO ARTIFICIAL INTELLIGENCE

A visit to Chichén Itza is always a fascinating experience. No surprise that it was voted in 2007 to become one of the New 7 Wonders of the World. Why has it disappeared? Even though the Spanish Empire conquered the last Mayan city in 1697, the decline began a long time earlier in the 9th century.

There had been a combination of reasons for the fall. Continuous warfare between the various extending cities let to resource depletion based on extending deforestation. Then in a next step to human-caused climate change on the Yucatan peninsula. More and more times, the expected rain did not come, and bad harvests had been the result.

This does not only remind to actual scenarios but also explains risks arising the operation of Artificial Intelligence (AI). For the Mayan population, their high priests had been comparable to today's AI. Supposedly in direct contact with the gods, they had been an enigmatic black box, predicting the future based on ceremonies and their interpretations. Part of the magic can be explained with science. Knowledgeable about mathematics and astronomy, they not only could predict lunar eclipses, but more importantly, the beginning of the seasons, including expected rainfalls, imperative for effective farming.

Like an AI, they analyzed the patterns of the past to predict the future. In the beginning, these patterns had been strong, but the slowly starting climate change made rain less predictable. As the priests interpreted the earlier patterns with divine creation and interference instead of a holistic understanding of nature, they had been unable to correctly interpret the destroyed patterns (action of prayer & sacrifice leading to the result of rain & good harvest). Due to the priests, the problem had been unsatisfied gods, so more human sacrifice should solve the situation. As it did not, civil unrests destroyed the society including the role of the actual high priests. Even though the Maya worshiped Mother Earth, they had been unable to identify the underlying cause of the perceived change; they had been unable to adapt and suffered a long decline.

Comparing a high priest to AI is an interesting thought, as both should resume and transport knowledge. One from the gods, one from the collected libraries of human knowledge. What is to learn? AI is based on data and statistics, it shall not be a black box, but transparent and auditable. This because the results of AI are perceived by humans, meaning the oversight and responsibility for the modern priest must be with the educated human society.

8.1 Tuvalu: Metaverse back to Dystopia

The nation of Tuvalu announced becoming the First Digital Nation.[63] In times of Digital Transformation, on the first view a positive message. Nevertheless, this announcement by Tuvaluan Minister Simon Kofe at the COP27 United Nations Climate Change Conference in Sharm el-Sheik was the complete opposite. Caused by rising sea levels, the country located in the

---

[63] Tuvalu (2027): "The First Digital Nation", https://www.tuvalu.tv

Polynesian part of the Pacific Ocean is at risk of disappearing. With his video message, Kofe explained that a country is more than just land, it is culture, heritage and vision. Accordingly, Tuvalu will upload all relevant information into the Cloud to recreate Tuvalu in the Metaverse.

Today, the Metaverse is marketed by tech companies as a positive vision of the future, but its origins came from the 1992 dystopian novel "Snow Crash", where author Neal Stephenson coined the expression for a first time.[64] Also the Ernest Cline's novel "Ready Player One" from 2011 was not meant as a positive prediction outlook.[65] Reality, in combination with the arts, brings the Metaverse now back to such darker scenarios.

Please see the impressive website "The First Digital Nation", about the digitalization of Te Afualiku Islet, the smallest island of Tuvalu, the first part of the country what will get lost, and accordingly, the first one to get digitalized. Without immediate, global climate action, all of Tuvalu will only exist in the Metaverse.

---

[64] Stephenson, Neal (1992): "Snow Crash"
[65] Cline, Ernest (2011): "Ready Player One"

9 TOMOIKI & GAMIFICATION

Being part of Governance, the Ethics & Compliance function is a relevant part of the ESG (Environmental, Social and Governance) concept. The organizational stakeholders understand the impact of the company on society and environment and chose to be a good corporate citizen. This on the one hand, is based on ethics and values, but also on the other hand based on economical understanding. As Professor Erich Gutenberg defined in 1979 it his "principle of profit", corporations in a market-based system are striving for to maximize their profit, based on the used resources, on the long-run.[66] The motivation of the need for good behavior is given, nevertheless, as employees' motivation can temporarily rise and fall, discipline apart is required. This also as "on the long run" has different meaning for an over hundred years old organization than typically for an individual employee, who plans on shorter terms, as for example, the acquisition of a new car, new house, marriage, university costs, etc.

Ethics & Compliance works in parallel on the two sides, the motivation, but also control. With the understanding why adequate behavior is required, also understanding of the controls get achieved. There is no one-fits-all approach, but in general, the focus should be on prevention, the motivational part.

---

[66] Gutenberg, Erich (1979): "Grundlagen der Betriebswirtschaftslehre, Band 1: Die Produktion"

Speaking about achieving a carbon neutral world, Mitsubishi Heavy Industry President and CEO Seiji Izumisawa relates to the traditional Japanese concept "Tomoiki", which can be translated as with "coexistence." This is not limited to the present but connecting employees and other stakeholders also with past and future, the company's history back to its founder and short- and long-term goals.[67]

Going a step further, the 2016 science fiction drama "Arrival", including the book it is based on, "Story of Your Life" by Ted Chiang, discussed the idea that past, present and future exist in parallel. Similar to the eyes, with which humans can observe their three dimensional environment, other (Alien) lifeforms may have a different sensor to also perceive their individual past and future. This is not related to destiny but based on their attitudes and decisions.

To ensure motivation, Ethics & Compliance must act as story-teller, not only explaining laws and regulations, but also the underlying insights why they had been created, this as they align to the vision of society or in the case of internal guidelines, directly to the company's founder. Furthermore, employees must understand what the consequence of their potential behavior will be. This can be related to society, company, their children or them personally. Often, analyzing a Compliance case from point of one single involved employee can have a higher impact on the audience than speaking about court decisions and millions of fines.

---

[67] Mitsubishi Heavy Industries (2023): "MISSION NET ZERO – How MHI will achieve carbon neutrality by 2040"

Cloud-technology enables companies to use gamification to tell the story. Inspired by classic Adventure- and Roleplay-games, and similar to the popular escape rooms, employees can face different scenarios, which develop based on the user's decisions. Users may repeat the scenarios to see how different decisions lead to different outcomes, including personal consequences. Relevant also to show that negative reactions often do not come directly after a bad decisions, but maybe one or various steps later.

Such games should not replace classic training and workshops but could work as efficient add-on. Depending on the organization's budget and technical possibilities, such games could be created in PowerPoint or elaborated on a Virtual Reality platform; even better is to organize it as teambuilding in a physical escape room. Generative AI can be used to create such games or discussion cases.

Assistant professor of psychology Rachel White explained: "Self-distancing gives us a little bit of extra space to think rationally about the situation." A perception of yourself as a separate person, like a character in a game, reduces emotional engagement, employees are able to logically analyze their behavior. Furthermore, a comparison with a situation where the same character acted correctly should make them understand that they have the capability to do so. This especially as adequate behavior, such as for example denying a bribe, stop bullying, etc., should not require being a super-hero.

Independent if reached via gamification or interactive discussions, these tools and events should support transporting the compliance message including how it aligns to ethics and sustainability. This knowledge about the impact of individual and corporate decisions should lead to higher empathy, as corruption is no faceless crime, but create victims up to killing people. Back to the philosophy of Tomoiki, aligning the mentioned knowledge with the imperative of coexistence, not only compliance, but all internal processes get aligned at the goal to minimize the organizational negative impact to create sustainability for company and society.

Continuous communication and dialogue is imperative, as companies do not strive for the perfect fit for today's business environment, but for tomorrow's. It means that companies are in constant flow and change. Due to this, employees are aware that the "go to market" could be improved, but do not see that the company decided against this based on its future vision. This may lead to frustration and temptation to deviate internal guidelines, up to external laws, especially if the company is active in higher risk regions with a relevant risk of impunity. To reduce the risk, Ethics & Compliance, as experts in change management, not only must explain the regulations and expected behavior, but must align this with explaining the company's vision of the future and how this not only benefits the organization, but also society in general ("tomoiko") and he individual employee. With this, EC can use information and knowledge to create understanding and empathy on the employee side. Change management changes from "push" (demand by management) to "pull" (requested by employees). Employees perceive a higher commitment and are motivated to protect the company, including following regulations and law.

10 EXAMPLE PERU: BUSINESS TRAVEL AS INSPIRATION FOR ETHICS & COMPLIANCE

"Disruption" means to stop the current and give opportunity for the new. Disruption does not automatically mean that something new will be implemented, but that a break can be used to think about the status quo and potential alternatives. A decision-making process will choose between continuing the known path or change to a new one. For an individual, regular disruptions are required to avoid a "tunnel vision" and related behavior risks. Even if working in the ethics and compliance field leads to a higher awareness, also such experts are not immune against ethical pitfalls or developing various biases.

Having a responsibility for Latin America is a fascinating task, as there are the known risks, but also exists a motivated workforce. Besides that, business travel can be combined with known tourist locations to take some days off and get disrupted by new experiences. One example is Peru, related to its Gross Domestic Product, the sixth largest economy in Latin America.

Being in the country's capital Lima, a one day trip can be used to visit the UNESCO World Heritage site of Caral. Even if already re-discovered in the beginning of the 20th century, only radiocarbon dating in early 2000s concluded that these pyramids are around 4,600 years old; making Caral, after Mesopotamia, the second oldest civilization on the planet. These are results which are not yet included in all history books. A reminder that also Compliance and business ethics are not fixed in stone, but newer ideas as system-thinking, link the functions to behavioral science and artificial intelligence, leading to holistic combinations like GRC (Governance, Risk & Compliance) and ESG (Environmental, Social & Governance). What is valid for a higher number of job functions, also applies for the Ethics & Compliance Officer, the job-profile in ten or even 20 years will be completely different from today. Curiosity and continues learning are required to stay up to date. Sometimes even knowledge must be unlearned to be replaced by new insights and theories.

A better known touristic attraction are the famous Nazca lines, being up 2,500 years old and up to 370 meters long. In their complete form, they are best visible from the sky, for example from a small airplane. Continuous lines are forming a figure, like a monkey, hummingbird, condor, whale, dog, or spider. For corporate employees it is often not possible to understand the connection of approval processes and controls with the overall process or even the company as total. Missing understanding can lead to conscious or subconscious deviation to processes, as they get perceived as a bureaucratic burden without offering a benefit. Accordingly, the Ethics & Compliance Officer has the duty to not only explain the punctual processes and tools but must elevate the employees with training or communication, so that they understand the complete holistic processes and their benefit for society, company and themselves.

The famous former Inca capital Cusco fascinates with its architecture, where new Spanish Colonial buildings had been erected on Inca bases with walls including perfectly drafted stones fitting without any kind of fillings (like cement) in between. A good example what Ethics & Compliance must reach, not being perceived as a foreign body, but an integrated and natural part of the organization. Of course, having the needed independence for decision-making, investigation, and whistleblower-protection, but besides that Compliance must be with the acknowledged company values, mission, and vision; a company culture lived by the employees.

Of course, open ears and eyes makes the traveler also aware of the negative impact of corruption on economy and society. Peru is on position 101 of the 2023 Transparency International Corruption Perception Index.

Even if not related to our Ethics & Compliance tasks, such travel experiences lead to inspiration and ideas, which could be implemented when back at the workplace. More than that, such trips in between can create awe moments. The acknowledged Cambridge Dictionary defines awe as "a feeling of great respect sometimes mixed with fear or surprise." Two-way respect is basic for business ethics. On the one hand, employees shall respect the company, including its underlying values, mission, and vision. On the other one, a company shall respect employees, who can get perceived by an honest and efficient Environmental, Social & Governance (ESG) system.

Respect is the base on which moment of awe can be created. Even Ethics & Compliance has the final purpose to reduce the financial risk of legal deviations or reputational damage, "respect" is base to win employees over, as protecting the individual employees also means protecting the company, and the other way around.

Business travel may include risks, especially if employees socialized in lower risk countries (related to corruption and safety) must travel to higher risk regions. Tailor-made travel training can reduce the risk and in parallel motivate the employee to be open and curious, if possible, also use the opportunity to take time off before or after the project or meeting to get to know country and culture. Information should lead to empathy and the understanding that corruption is no faceless crime; and furthermore, prepare employees to decline bribery and even small facilitation payments. Besides leisure, travel is beneficial for the business, as external stakeholders appreciate interest in the culture and better understanding reduces the risk of frictions. Furthermore, travel can create awe moments.

Awe leads to more happiness, and a higher employee satisfaction to a higher perceived accountability of everyone to protect the organization against reputational and financial damage. Even if travel is a perfect opportunity to create awe moments, such can be created also at the employee's home location. In alignment with the ESG philosophy, companies seek to participate in national or international community engagement events. The focus is on giving back, and the support of environment and society. Nevertheless, the joined effort to work on such a project is also a team-building effect and when the goal gets achieved, employees perceive an awe-moment, as combing individual and company values let to a win-win-win situation, including the community.

The US American author and philosopher Ayn Rand defined once: *"Achievement of your happiness is the only moral purpose of your life, and that happiness, not pain or mindless self-indulgence, is the proof of your moral integrity, since it is the proof and the result of your loyalty to the achievement of your values."*

ABOUT THE AUTHOR

Patrick Henz is the Head of Governance, Risk & Compliance at a leading engineering and plant construction company. He drives an effective GRC system combining integrity, respect, passion, and sustainability. Responsibilities include Business Resilience and Community Engagement. He promotes holistic sustainability strategy, speaks at workshops and conferences. President of Honor at Marcus Evans' Latin-American Corporate Compliance Conference in 2011 and 2012. Panelist at The Economist Mexico Summit 2015. Co-founder of Ethics & Compliance Forum Mexico, editor, and co-author of Ethics & Compliance Manual. Co-chair at "MedicReS AI 2023 International Congress on Good Artificial Intelligence Practice & Innovation in Health Sciences." Author of "Business Philosophy according to Enzo Ferrari" and "Tomorrow's Business Ethics: Dick vs. Deming."

www.ingramcontent.com/pod-product-compliance
Lightning Source LLC
Chambersburg PA
CBHW071100290526
45795CB00004B/1584

* 9 7 9 8 8 8 2 7 8 4 2 7 9 *